A Collection of Advice

*from Social Media*

# Thaye Dorje
*His Holiness the 17th Gyalwa Karmapa*

# A Collection of Advice
from Social Media

RABSEL
Éditions

*First Edition:*
*Shri Diwakar Publications, India, 2015*

*Copyright © Shri Diwakar Publications, India*


*Second Edition:*
© Rabsel Éditions, La Remuée, 2017
ISBN 979-10-93883-14-4

www.rabseleditions.com

# Table of Contents

I

# Preface

The Collection of Advice from Social Media unites the words of wisdom that H.H. Karmapa Trinley Thaye Dorje has shared on his Facebook page in a small book. Even in this era where we have access to all kinds of information by the means of the internet, there are people who prefer to rely on books for guidance. It might be especially helpful for people who are in need of advice about a specific problem since the book covers a wide range of topics and gives a short but deep teaching about each of them.

We are very fortunate to have the opportunity to publish this book with the blessing of His Holiness.

Sri Diwakar Publications, October 20th 2015

# Why Do We Need to Produce Compassion?

Very simply, because every sentient being is kind; every sentient being is innately compassionate. So there is already a fundamental reason to do so, although at the moment it may feel difficult. But during the space of our practice, such boundaries are not there. You have your own space of practice, and in that practice you can really combine both your friends and foes together. It is a perfect space when we meditate.

# What Is the Best Practice for Working with Speech?

I like that question—it is quite simple and to the point.

I think a simple answer would be that any speech that comes from a kind heart (in the unemotional sense) would help make it more like Buddha-speech.

If someone is a little bit emotionally disturbed and shaken, then the speech expressed may reflect these internal disturbances, and this may in turn be confused for a kind heart. A kind heart flows not from emotion, but from a clear conscience. When the conscience is clear, the heart is kind and beneficial speech and activities follow. When the conscience is clear, the speech becomes more like Buddha-speech.

I believe that the reason why we call it "Buddha-speech" is because there is simply no agenda at all. We can see this from the very sutras that we have; the very teachings and actual words of Buddha reflect this. It is pure generosity, it is genuine sharing—the ultimate form of sharing.

There is a saying that sharing is loving. In this case,

the Buddha's teachings are the perfect example of this. Buddha's genuine sharing is a reflection of limitless love.

So what are the qualities of Buddha-speech? Having perfected not only speech, but action and thought over many eons (basically meaning over many, many life-times) where there is simply no need for any agenda—as one can see the faults within any kind of agenda, seeing the positive qualities of generosity and a kind heart, and then simply sharing knowledge.

Let me give an example. I think most of you are familiar with the various aspiration prayers. One that comes to my mind is that of the Samantabhadra Aspiration Prayer. It is perfect in every way. There is simply not one sentence—in fact, not one word or even one syllable—that is not a Buddha-speech. (Unless, of course, it has been wrongly interpreted or written in some way).

Of course, all of the sutras and the teachings of Buddha are examples of Buddha-speech. They are perfect because there is no self-interest, agenda, or expectation of something in return. It is pure giving. It is genuine sharing.

Going back to the characteristics of Buddha-speech, an important question to ask is if something is beneficial. Speaking about the weather, for example, may not be particularly useful (except in certain circumstances). If speech is beneficial, if it is useful, then it is worth considering. Otherwise, it may be better to leave it. Understanding the context is important, as some things may be beneficial in some cases but useless in others, and vice versa. It is also important to consider how much control we have over our speech, thoughts and actions—how much composure do we have as an individual?

There are times when one can engage in various speeches, engage in various topics. Whether it is talking about the weather, painting, cooking, baking, sports—whatever—it doesn't matter so much, as long as it is beneficial.

But what does it mean for speech to be beneficial? From a Buddhist point of view, when we use the term "beneficial," it often refers to two things: beneficial in this life and the next life. Beneficial speech will help us reach liberation and then gain *Samyakasambuddaya*.

So if it helps an individual and others, we can engage in seemingly pointless speech. We can whistle, hum, whatever—as long as it is beneficial. Maybe, for some people they like to hum—maybe humming is their hobby! Maybe it is their passion; maybe it is the thing that really makes their day. If they are not able to hum that day, for them it is a bad day. They may not be able to sleep properly; they might have nightmares.

For someone like this, it might be helpful to encourage them by humming along with them, to help them reach liberation and enlightenment! You hum a little and you get closer, when you hum twice even closer, and a little more to a point where one can maybe have a conversation! Yes, understanding the context and what is truly beneficial is very important.

# Learning Which Kind of Knowledge
# Has the Most Benefit

The values that expand our view beyond ourselves and our material concerns. These non-material values are key to the development of human beings. According to myself, developing our consciousness, our understanding, is the best investment in life that we can make: education shapes our minds. If we don't teach values and nurture Inner Wealth, then when there is a crisis, we often find that first and foremost there is a crisis of values.

The purpose of our life is much more than to survive, much more than sustaining the physical body—it is to help develop consciousness. The emphasis and direction of education should therefore not just be about accumulating information to serve outer wealth, but to help develop consciousness, to help young people nurture their innate values of wisdom and compassion for the benefit of society.

# Learning from the Lehman Brothers

Saturday, September 15 marks four years since the fall of the Lehman brothers, the beginning of the economic crisis. Seeing and experiencing how the economic system has caused pain and sorrow for many people around the world, we cannot forget, however, that it was once intended for something good and to benefit everybody. With the economy as well as our day-to-day lives, we have to remember to combine the qualities of compassion and wisdom with everything we do.

Since I first started travelling almost fourteen years ago, I have visited a great many different countries. While all my travels taught me a lot, this year's European tour, "The Wealth of Europe," was particularly educational.

I met with many young people, including some young ambassadors of the Prince's Trust, and listened to what they are going through, how they feel about life, about the present economic situation, and also how they perceive the future.

We are all connected. What I've also understood through all these interactions is that as long as we were born as human beings and live in this world, then no matter what kind of life we lead, we are all very much connected with all individuals and all societies of the world, so we cannot run away from worldly responsibilities and circumstances.

Even for myself, a Buddhist teacher who tries to follow the path of Buddha Shakyamuni, it is crucial to be aware of and connected with whatever is happening in the world.

With this in mind, I set up the Wealth of Europe Initiative. Over 700 young Europeans have shared their concerns, aspirations and priorities in a poll over the last 10 weeks. The results of the poll clearly showed that the vast majority of young people rate non-material values far higher than material wealth. Based on what I have learned from the Buddha's teachings, I had already expected these kinds of results. Nevertheless, they were very encouraging for me and gave me a lot of hope and inspiration.

Positive qualities lie within us. No matter how challenging things may seem at times when we look at the state of the world, there is always hope and a way to overcome these challenges. Seeing the potential of young people in particular, all we need to do is share and communicate.

By communicating and sharing our thoughts, the positive qualities that we all have naturally emerge. Without communication we may have all kinds of positive means and ideas, but they lie dormant. However, once we start communicating, even the smallest of means becomes so vital and so effective.

We don't have to put ourselves under pressure to change or reform the world; through awareness, as well as constant and clear communication we can have a holistic view and perspective of the world. We can take the simple example of the Wealth of Europe Initiative: a few thoughts and insights were shared that raised awareness for the wealth of Europe through the lens of young people.

With awareness, we naturally know that we have to focus on our inner wealth—that our inner qualities are among the most important factors in having a meaningful life. Through these qualities we will also have the wisdom of knowing how to go about material values, to what extent we have to utilise material wealth, and how to do so responsibly.

I hope that through further communication all of us will be able to bring awareness all over the world, to help learn and apply the lessons of the past.

# What Does It Take to Be a Peace Ambassador?

It might feel like a very grand title, one that govern-ments or large organizations might use. We might think of ambassadors traveling the world, spreading a mes-sage, visiting places of conflict. While this is certainly true in some cases, there is a different—but equally im-portant—type of ambassador.

In life, it is somehow easier to think of peace as being needed somewhere on the other side of the world. It is the responsibility of diplomats, charities and large orga-nizations—how could we possibly have a role?

Meaningful peace starts much closer to home. Mean-ingful peace benefits those directly in front of us. What is the point of promoting peace in one part of the world if we leave those directly around us feeling upset? Mean-ingful peace needs us all to be ambassadors for peace. Right here. Right now.

Fortunately, we all have the tools already to be Peace

Ambassadors. Being an ambassador for peace does not require special training, experience, or a title. Being an ambassador for peace means tapping into your own innate values—your inner wealth—and using them to benefit those closest to you. It means being alive, awake, taking responsibility for your actions. It means not being driven by your emotions, but controlling them.

But how? Well, the first step is to recognize that we all affect the people around us by our thoughts, words and actions. Those people will influence others through their thoughts, words and actions. These personal encounters and influences are magnified in communities, on social networks, until very quickly millions of people are touched in some way. So the first step is to recognize that in today's society we all have the power to be a global peace ambassador through the people closest to us. I think straight away of my family and my students.

They make a difference to me, and I also make a difference to them. We can all affect people positively or negatively, towards or away from peace. Peace starts with our own thoughts, words and actions.

Now that we have this power for peace, and we realise that it is not the sole power of big organizations and governments, it is important that we use this power to benefit others. Sometimes, when there are difficulties, it is difficult to smile, and to try and bring positivity to yourself and those around you. It might be beneficial to reflect for a moment on the most important people in your life. Reflect on their kindness, the sacrifices they have gone through at times to express that kindness. When we appreciate these people, we may also be inspired to show kindness, to share a smile, even when it feels hardest to do so. So it's not about doing years and years of work and finally bringing something called peace. It's not like that. Peace is now.

So on Peace Day, September 21, I appeal to all people to be ambassadors for peace—a meaningful peace that starts within us, and with those directly in front of us.

On this day, I share my heartfelt wishes for all people to nurture their innate values of compassion and wisdom, and for all to reflect on and appreciate the kindness of others. And I share my heartfelt wishes that one day, every day will be a day of peace.

# Mindfulness

When you have mindfulness, then whatever you want to achieve—for example if you want to construct something—you will make sure that the construction is perfect. If you do not have mindfulness, even though you may want to achieve something amazing, you may miss something crucial, so if there is an obstacle it may collapse. With mindfulness, everything is protected. There is no room for error, so that no matter what, whether there is an earthquake or some other obstacle in life, the foundation and building stands firm.

# Equanimity

Equanimity helps the mind to be stable and calm. So what we do is bring in our mind all of the favorable circumstances, unfavorable circumstances, favorable friends, unfavorable friends—bring them all together and then just try to view all of them as neutral, middle ground.

This then gives the mind some time to relax, to have focus. Only then can we attempt to practice compassion and loving kindness, and of course gradually the sympathetic joy, or the part where we can rejoice.

# Is Understanding Fear Beneficial?

Fear. We all experience it. We might feel anxious about our loved ones, our self-esteem, growing old, or even dying. Or we might read the news, see stories of violence, tragedies on India's roads or railways, details of the latest health scare.

What we fear varies according to who we are as individuals, and the environment we live in. In a society driven by competition, we might be fearful of not keeping up with our peers, our neighbors, or colleagues.

In a culture driven by the accumulation of material wealth, we might fear the feeling of not having "enough," or not having as much money as others.

Such fears are extremely common. The good news is that experiencing fear is not a bad thing—it means that you are alive. But being overwhelmed by fear is something different.

**Fear in Buddhism:**
Buddha himself, before he reached enlightenment, experienced fear like everyone else. He, too, feared growing old, falling ill, and dying.

But he realised that fear is like a self-fulfilling prophecy—without understanding the cyclic nature of this world, that which we fear will keep on repeating itself.

If we fear something in this moment, in this life—and fail to truly understand it—the same pattern will repeat itself in future moments, in future lives.

In Buddhist terms, only when we liberate ourselves from the causes (karma - causal actions, and *kleśas* - afflictive emotions), conditions (habitual patterns and tendencies), and effects (the various existences) of fear, can we begin to overcome it.

The idea of overcoming afflictive emotions and non-virtuous actions might sound easier said than done. But our future depends on it. For there is a greater type of fear that could undermine everything that is good in our world. This fear, or perhaps more accurately "terror," is born when we give in to our negative emotions, and dismiss the universal law of karma and causality. When we have no belief in cause and effect, when we ignore the cyclic nature of fear and of life itself, then we are able to commit all kinds of atrocities. When we give in to our fear, we shake the foundations of virtue, and risk losing the moral fabric of our society. When we fail to understand fear, fear becomes our foe.

**Overcoming Fear by Understanding Fear:**
Fortunately, as human beings, we have a unique advantage when it comes to overcoming fear.

Other sentient beings, such as animals, experience

fear and other emotions, but they are limited only to the five senses. Humans, however, can utilise logic, reasoning, and particularly our inner qualities, such as the mind looking inwardly, and try to examine and understand what fear is.

Understanding fear and overcoming it are one and the same thing. Fear itself derives from a lack of knowledge and understanding—about the "unknown." The solution, therefore, lies in understanding fear—not to get rid of it, but to recognise it as a part of life, and to try to channel it for positive means. When we understand fear, fear becomes our friend.

Human beings have a unique choice and opportunity to overcome fear. We may not always see this choice, particularly in the moments when we feel afraid, but it is there. Whether we use this opportunity is up to us.

One of the worst things about not understanding fear is that it can waste time, which is so precious. If we have a non-virtuous attitude, or fail to understand the true nature of our emotions, fear can accumulate until it is overwhelming. We feel defeated. From a Buddhist perspective, in that moment we have forgotten that compassion exists, that compassion will prevail—and in this forgotten moment, our fear is compounded.

### Channeling Fear for Loving Kindness:

When we approach fear with a virtuous attitude, we can use reasoning and logic to overcome it. Whether it is through meditation, talking to loved ones, or other ways, we are able to uncover the "unknown," and take away fear's power. When we examine fear, we discover a simple and powerful truth: fear is neither good nor bad. Fear is neutral. What is positive or negative is our response and relationship to fear—how we understand it, approach it, channel it. It's like any other tool that we can find in life. We discover that fear does not inherently exist—if it did, we would not experience peace or compassion at all.

When we understand that it is us, and not our emotions, that have the power, we are able to channel our fear in a positive way. Understanding fear helps us to be decent, kind and caring people. And by being a kind person, with a good heart, we are also able to face fear more easily. This kind of virtuous circle, or karmic cycle, holds great hope for humanity.

In Buddhist terms, all of the problems in our society stem from a lack of understanding, a fear of the unknown. When we challenge this ignorance through logic, through reasoning, through tapping into our boundless internal resources of wisdom and compassion, we manifest hope—not just for ourselves, but for our world. Understanding fear implies that we understand ourselves. If we understand fear, then we understand more about compassion, about what it means to be human.

Perhaps the greatest benefit of facing fear and overcoming it is that we do not waste time. In fact, we use our fear to focus more on the precious present. We all know that we face serious challenges, in India and all around the world. Let us not waste a moment, for every moment is an opportunity. Let us face our fears with courage, with understanding, and with loving kindness for all sentient beings.

# Finding Balance: A Public Question

*"Realisation of impermanence is an important part of building the motivation to practice. However, lay people are still mostly caught up with work and family, and the time left for Dharma study, inner reflection, and meditation becomes little. Should we consciously try to limit the time spent on work by getting a less hectic job and "[trying]" not to get married—which will increase family commitments— just so we have time to practice?*

*Practice I feel is very important, but, if we continue to live on beyond our next breath, bread and butter, family and friends, are also important.*

*The current day and age does not allow us to be like Milarepa and be so extreme as to survive on nettles alone. What is your advice to us lay people as to how to balance practice and our mundane lives?"*

First of all, we have to be aware of the value of practice. I think the person who asks this question seems to understand the value of it.

For other people, in order to decide how to balance such things, and also to understand the answers, I think it is important to know the value of Buddha dharma.

Knowing the value of Buddha dharma is deeply connected with knowing the value of other people, and the connection with them. Now in this case, the person asks about family—which is directly related to Buddha Dharma. So in some ways, the idea of separating family time and time to practice is a little bit more complicated than it first seems.

So first of all one has to really understand the value and meaning of the Buddha dharma. The next step is to ask the following question: "What can I do, according to where I am right now, according to my own circumstances, and my own time?"

This question is all about managing time, so again we may ask ourselves, "What can I manage?" Of course, we have to look at it quite realistically in terms of what is manageable, and also in terms of what is necessary and what is unnecessary. There may be a lot of things that we spend our time on that are quite unnecessary, and I think we then have to find the courage to be able to somehow slowly, slowly let go of these unnecessary activities.

These could vary from one individual to another. For some, maybe painting is beneficial; maybe it is a way to somehow benefit oneself and others. For others, it might be a complete distraction, so accordingly we have to see. What is required is an honest exploration into what can be done, what can be managed, and what is necessary and beneficial.

So I think if we cover these areas, then we are able to challenge this idea that there isn't enough time. Indeed, just by going through these questions, we are actually making time—we are already making progress. At the very least, we develop a deeper understanding of our situation.

Once we have covered these questions, then I think we are left with the last step. This is to plan our life so that we are able to do everything that is necessary and beneficial. In this case, we have to make time to practice; we have to make time for others; we have to do everything, and somehow make it quite balanced, equal. It is difficult to find this balance, but it is important to plan in this way. It is also important to remember that the Buddha dharma reaches into all aspects of our life and experiences, and our connections with others, so in some ways every moment is also an opportunity to practice and to find balance.

# How Can Buddhism Help in Our Current Crisis?

That's a very good question. Of course global warming is a real issue, but from time to time I feel that maybe the idea of this threat is a little bit overused. When this threat is overused, it can lead to the feeling that there is very little an individual can do, which is not beneficial—or true.

What is needed is the knowledge about what each of us can do in any situation, and I believe Buddhism has a very important role here.

In this context, "knowledge" is not just a vague term, but refers to something very particular: the knowledge of our inner qualities—our inner knowledge. In other words, a type of knowledge that helps to unlock a hundred doors at the same time. This is the intention of the Buddha Dharma. In this sense, I think we are already in a beneficial position to address all kinds of challenges.

When we think of knowledge in more general terms, the usual method and form that it takes is education. If we leave aside the Buddhist part for a moment, I think that in many cases around the world, the emphasis on education today is much better than previously in history. There are, of course, still challenges faced today, but in many cases, where there was previously an absence of education opportunities, now there is an abundance of it. In fact, there are so many education opportunities in some parts of the world, that sometimes there is a problem of not knowing which route to take, a problem of choice.

As knowledge is what is required to tackle global warming and other challenges, I believe that education provides a very good platform for this knowledge and potential to be cultivated.

Education from a Buddhist point of view—what I would like to call "inner wealth," the unborn qualities that we all have, and which I already mentioned in my first answer—is about cultivating knowledge and qualities that are already there. No one had to teach us them; no one had to open our eyes or expose us to anything like that. Somehow, these qualities are naturally there, such as being kind, being generous, being understanding... one could even say the most basic of qualities.

These are the things that I think we need to tap into, and I think that is key to what Buddhism can offer. Ever since our historical Buddha Shakyamuni taught the Buddha dharma, these were His very first words and also more or less His last words too. And ever since, the Buddha Dharma that we have been practicing over the centuries and millennia, it has always been about cultivating our inner qualities. And whoever has understood this point has live [an amazing, extraordinary life]. Whoever they touched, whoever they met, whoever they spoke to—there was always a benefit.

One great example would be that of Milarepa. If we just look at his life story we can see that whoever he met, whatever the context, after that meeting, somehow there was always a benefit, even from simple accidents.

So I think that in terms of overcoming global challenges, Buddhism has a great deal to offer. The platform is already there, the methods to cultivate our inner wealth, and so all we need to do is just act upon it. But how?

In this very moment, this very space that we have right here, right now, there is an opportunity. This moment for us is the center of the universe, nowhere else. So here and now we can already start doing something. In other words, the Buddha dharma provides us the important knowledge and understanding about what each of us can do in any situation. So there is somehow no need to feel helpless or hopeless, because each of us can do so much.

In this case, the fortunate thing is that we have to hardly move a muscle to achieve so much. We just need to focus on recognizing what these inner qualities are, or what this inner wealth is—just by sitting. Buddha found a way where basically we seemingly need to do hardly anything. Whatever we're doing, whether we are sitting, talking, or even sleeping, we can activate and cultivate these inner qualities of wisdom and compassion.

If we can follow in the footsteps of Buddha, then we will be able to stop global warming, ice age, stone age, everything—all in a single sitting.

# What Do I Say to Mother Who is Dying of Cancer, and How Can I Help Her?

I believe that when anyone is in this kind of condition—be it cancer or any other form of illness—in these difficult moments, I think there is only one thing that we can provide. In fact, we can provide this, not just during difficult times, but also when things are seemingly alright. What is this thing? Our countless inner qualities.

Now, in this case, providing emotional support is priceless. It is the best—there is nothing of greater value. At such a moment, whatever amazing things we can provide materialistically will not help at all. At such a moment, power; fame; material wealth doesn't matter—instead that simple gesture of emotional support goes a long way. It is everything.

This is particularly true when it comes from someone whom you know, for it is easier for the recipient to accept.

There are cases, of course, when a stranger gives

that kind of support, and this also helps. However, in the case of the person asking the question, I think the best thing you can offer is the time and energy to give emotional support. Even if it is challenging, it may be beneficial for you to appear and express in front of the patient that you are alright, that you are strong and you are confident—confident that everything will be alright—and then of course also express this through verbal and physical gestures.

And then I think there are some cases where the patient may become cured. But even if they don't, at least they will be able to go through that journey in a much more peaceful manner.

Yes, these are the things that the Buddha dharma can always provide.

# Pain, Gain, and the Race of Life

This summer, the world is looking towards London to celebrate its athletes. For them, the saying "no pain, no gain" is part of their path to excellence. For the rest of us, we might be left wondering whether all this pain is necessary. Wouldn't life be much easier if we only had gain?

Nobody wants pain and crises, but in life, it is inevitable that we will go through such experiences. They are a general part of life—there is no life without pain. In fact, from a Buddhist perspective there is a lot of truth in the saying "no pain, no gain," though maybe not exactly in terms of how it is usually understood.

How to make it work for you? If we know how to use our wisdom in dealing with the pain and difficulties we go through, such experiences can help us develop greater understanding and inner wealth.

1. Accept that pain is a natural part of life: from time to time we will go through pain, emotional turmoil and crises, simply because all of these are part and parcel of our human existence.

Therefore, understanding that, however hard we might try, we cannot exactly avoid such experiences, we might as well accept them and learn something from them. However hard we might try to avoid the inevitable, when we accept and attempt to understand painful experiences, we can learn and grow.

2. Pain and joy are—like light and darkness—two sides of the same medal. They are interdependent and inseparably connected to each other. When painting a picture or taking a photograph, if there is no light and no darkness, there is no picture and there is no painting. It is the very contrast of light and darkness that brings out the beauty and the colour.

Similarly, since we do have a life, there is no point in saying that we want a life without problems and crises. That would be just like saying that we would like to have a picture without light and darkness. To take this train of thought further, from that perspective even life itself seems to be dependent on death, too. There is no life without death—and the opposite is equally true.

This kind of understanding can really help us appreciate this experience called life—and appreciate the opportunities that we have to help ourselves and help others.

3. Wake up, wise up: whenever we face any form of crisis and apply our wisdom to it, pain has the ability to make us aware of our physical and mental state—

like a kind of wake-up call. Even though we might not be exactly happy about the pain, we can then find a way of appreciating the experience. Rather than focusing exclusively on getting rid of the pain as quickly as possible we are able to extract something meaningful from those feelings.

We all have a mind, and there is no mind without wisdom. Let us use our wisdom meaningfully, to see the nature of life, rather than using it to try to see a painting without light or shade.

However, in order to bring out our inherent wisdom, we really have to allow ourselves a moment to contemplate. By extracting anything that is helpful for our minds, we can help ourselves and help others. We don't need to move mountains. It is so simple— all we have to do is share our experience.

When we embrace pain as part of the mosaic of our life experiences, we gain a new perspective on life and the world—and get ahead together in the race of life.

# Are Wars of Words Violent?

The so-called war of words involving North Korea, South Korea, and the United States raises an important question for our time: how do we define violence?

Many people have pointed to the threat of violent conflict, but I believe that it has already taken place. In Buddhism, violence is thought of not just as physical action, but in terms of our thoughts and words as well. We can see through history that physical conflict rarely takes place without violent thoughts and words preceding them. Our thoughts manifest our words. Our words manifest our deeds.

As Buddha Shakyamuni, the founder of Buddhism says, "Words have the power to both destroy and heal. When words are both true and kind, they can change our world."

In the face of so much conflict, how can we manifest a world that heals, rather than destroys?

In many ways, conflicts are inevitable as we are living in an ever-changing world; they are part of our life. How we approach them, and whether we respond to them in a violent or nonviolent way, is very important. From a Buddhist perspective, ignorance is believed to be the original cause of conflict. Can you think of a conflict that has not in some way flowed from a lack of understanding or misunderstanding? Whether the conflict is little or large, the cause is not a mystery, but an aggregate of small misunderstandings accumulated over time.

If conflicts and misunderstandings are not tackled, disturbing emotions such as anger, hatred, and attachment lead to confusion. And where does confusion lead? To wars of words, to physical conflict.

The solutions to conflicts, whether in North Korea, or in our own minds, lies in understanding. There have been many reports and suggestions about the importance of dialogue between North Korea, South Korea, and the United States, but little attention has been paid to what dialogue is really for—to build understanding. There is no need for complicated solutions or cumbersome ideas. Sometimes these can be expressed through confusing or even violent phrases like "diplomatic offensive." Instead, we can apply simple logic and enter into an honest effort to understand one another.

I believe that this understanding is an inherent quality. Within all of us is a limitless pool, an inner wealth, that we can tap into to help calm the mind. This inner wealth is vast, with all of the understanding that we will ever need. There are many ways that we can access or reveal this inner wealth: through meditation, contemplation, or simply trying to breathe and calm the mind.

When we do this, we take an important step down a nonviolent path. As the great Hindu leader Gandhi Ji once said, "We may never be strong enough to be entirely nonviolent in thought, word and deed. But we must keep nonviolence as our goal and make strong progress towards it."

Some might say that it is easier said than done. But when we realize how closely related thinking, saying, and doing are, it is better to speak a word of peace than to say nothing at all.

# Where Is There Hope in the Face of Violence?

When we look into the events on that day, behind the smoke and destruction, we see numerous acts of compassion. Emergency services, volunteers, people of all backgrounds stretching out their hands and hearts to help each other. The human heart, Bodhicitta, is the most precious of all. While Buddhas are helpful in life, the compassionate heart is even more precious than a Buddha. In the human heart, we see limitless hope.

September 11th also marks the anniversary of when Mohandas Gandhi started the modern nonviolent movement. On this day in 1906, Satyagraha, the force of love or truth which flows from nonviolence, was born. This compassionate movement inspired Martin Luther King Jr, and countless others, to follow a nonviolent path. This compassionate movement lifted up the preciousness of the human heart, and the hope that flows from kindness. As Gandhi said, "Non-violence, which is the quality of the heart, cannot come by an appeal to the brain."

On this day, I appeal to your hearts, remember those who suffer. On this day, I appeal to your hearts: let compassion flow.

Gautama Buddha said, "Better than a thousand hollow words is one word that brings peace."

On this day, I appeal to your precious human hearts; may you share words that bring peace to all sentient beings.

# What Kind of Happiness Are You Seeking?

How much do we really know about happiness? From a Buddhist perspective, all sentient beings, including animals, seek happiness. We have a subconscious instinct to seek happiness—even though many of us don't have a clear idea what it is or how to achieve it.

From a Buddhist perspective, there are two types of happiness: emotional happiness and timeless happiness. emotional happiness could be described as seeking relief from the cold, or searching for sources of earning, position, or status. Although there is nothing wrong with this type of "worldly" happiness, when we reflect on it, we might understand that all of these examples, by their very nature, are temporary. Emotional happiness does not last. Therefore, timeless happiness becomes something very important to seek.

## Timeless Happiness

Timeless happiness is gained from understanding our own inherent qualities, such as compassion and loving kindness, and gaining wisdom about our true nature. When we reflect on the nature of this type of happiness, we find something unchanging, permanent - and therefore worthwhile to seek.

We might find ourselves confused about timeless Happiness. We are, after all, so closely connected to emotional Happiness, and get an instant reward from it every day. Timeless happiness might sound noble, even wonderful, but is it visible, attainable in everyday life? Actually, yes.

## Happiness in Family

My late grandmother led a very simple life, as a mother to my father. But the way she lived her life is something that will stay with me always, and is perhaps my greatest personal example of timeless happiness. Without having particular responsibilities that one might consider "amazing" or "newsworthy," but simply by being a mother, just practicing loving kindness, and other basic qualities of life, and of herself; what I witnessed is that no matter who approached her, no matter what kind of situations she was in, she had an unaltering attitude towards life. Whomever she met, she had the attitude of kindness and care—just like a mother. Visibly, you could see it; verbally, you could hear it. All of her words were extremely warm and gentle. And of course, all of these qualities stemmed from her own consciousness.

As Karmapa, I, of course, lead my life as a spiritual practitioner, but I learn so much from the way she carried herself, the way she carried her attitude to life. This memory for me is very precious because it helps remind me that timeless happiness is visible and evident in all of us. The happiness we are seeking is already here. So this example always helps me, always puts a smile on my face and in my heart.

## Buddha and Happiness

I am sure that every one of you have similar experiences, memories, that you can recall. From a Buddhist perspective, it is said that the potential, the seed, and the quality of true happiness or enlightenment are all there within every sentient being's centre.

Therefore, it is important not to consider timeless happiness as something that is distant or unattainable, or something to be celebrated on special occasions and put on the shelf for the rest of the year. Instead, timeless happiness is something that we can really get involved in, take part in, no matter what type of life we are living, no matter what type of conditions we might have. But first we have to notice it.

The benefit from taking the first step of achieving timeless happiness is captured in the word "timeless" itself. From a Buddhist perspective, the benefits are noble, decent, and virtuous from the very beginning. It is noble, decent, and virtuous in the middle. And it is noble, decent, and virtuous at the end as well—not just in this life, not just later on, but until the end, until we have given full rise, full realisation to timeless happiness.

From a Buddhist viewpoint, the best example of this unchanging happiness would be none other than Buddha himself. Buddha means "enlightened being," a fully awakened being. Now if we reflect on the way he sought and ultimately achieved timeless happiness, it is the same as we are doing today: reflecting on and examining the causes and conditions of happiness.

## The Happiness Exam

The only way in which we can truly examine happiness is by looking deep into ourselves: our way of being; the way we carry ourselves; our everyday behaviour and habits. By doing so, it helps us understand more about ourselves. If we understand more about ourselves, we understand more about others.

All of us have the basic qualities to attain happiness, we all share the potential—simply because we all have consciousness. We all have the same wish and aspirations as we are all searching for happiness.

If you look at Buddha's life story, it is clear that he could have had, and indeed he did have, everything he could wish for from worldly life. But after examining it, he could see that—no matter how pleasant or satisfactory a feeling or situation he was experiencing—these were all temporary. He saw that it was not the ultimate goal or priority to attain this type of experience, what we are calling emotional happiness. Therefore, he left that life in search of something that is lasting, something that is unchangeable. This is what students of Buddha's way and path are practicing: the practice of timeless happiness.

Having said all of this, to seek happiness, do we need to suddenly change the way we live? Do we need to renounce and abandon things from our lives? We may naturally have these kind of questions and doubts. I would say that it is all about the attitude—how we want to live our lives. It all depends on our priority, our ultimate goal. If our priority is to seek timeless happiness, the first thing we must do is reflect.

For five minutes a day everyday, it is beneficial to reflect on what we are really seeking, the conditions that we have been gathering, and the methods that we have been applying. There is no harm in taking a little time every day from our schedules. We can start by taking just five minutes a day—it's not much—and the practice itself doesn't need to involve intensive methods or rigorous procedures. All we need to do is sit, or stand in a place where we feel comfortable, quiet, and peaceful.

Then, simply meditate and reflect, with a calm state of mind and body. Reflect on the past 24 hours—nothing more; reflect on exactly what has happened. Do this in an unemotional way, without judgment. By doing so, there is so much benefit. You will understand more about yourself, the various interesting aspects of your life. Not only will this help your memory, gain clarity, but it can truly help you understand yourself, and the true nature of happiness.

I encourage all of you to try this. I follow this practice as much as I can, and it definitely brings a lot of benefit. It helps me to understand exactly where I am, what I have experienced in the past, and by doing so it also helps me understand what may happen, the possibilities. In this way, this simple practice can help us understand the past, the present, and the future. We feel confident, and can gain an insight into happiness.

I hope this is beneficial to all of you. I offer my aspirations and prayers that we all are able to achieve timeless Happiness. I pray that we will all gain clarity, and that we will all find the conditions to appreciate the connection that we have. I pray that we cultivate the conditions to realise the potential that we have, the bond that we all share such as the bond of family, the bond of friends. And I pray that this will grow not just emotional happiness, but timeless happiness in our world.

# Finding Freedom

Most of us tend to think about freedom as being able to say and do what we want. We think of freedom as depending on external circumstances. If we can't do what we want, we think, this is largely due to society's constraints on us.

So, naturally, we think of "others" as the enemies of freedom. In this way, we create a dualistic perspective, and, as a result, freedom becomes mostly about challenging our enemies, our foes... and about overcoming them.

But then, after some time, we might have some doubts, and we might start to ask ourselves, "Is this what freedom is really about?" The very nature of this outward perspective is that such doubts would keep popping up. Why? Because it is endless; because the actual source has not been dealt with. So how do we actually find true freedom?

For me, the Buddhist viewpoint is so interesting because it actually deals with the core of the problem. It focuses not only outwardly, but also on an inner perspective, on trying to know ourselves.

Right now, we may think that we are free do what we want, but actually we are not. We are totally dependent, totally dependent on so many things.

First and foremost, we are dependent on food, of course, because if we go really hungry we may become ill, and we may end up doing regrettable things. So, already on this primal level, we are dependent.

But it doesn't stop there. Even in our modern, well-developed societies, where so many of our basic needs are already taken care of and where most of us don't have to worry about these basic human needs, we are still dependent.

Most of all, we are dependent on our emotions. For example, whenever we experience fear, then we naturally go back to anger for support because anger seems like the only way to defend ourselves—so once again, we are dependent.

And so that's why, if we really sit down and think about it, we come to realize that we have no control over so many things, and at that point we actually experience just how powerless we are.

So, again, how can we achieve true freedom? In Buddhism, the power of freedom lies in controlling what we do, not the action itself. Genuine freedom is about gaining control of ourselves; gaining control of our bodies and speech initially, but above all, our minds.

From this point of view, freedom comes from knowing our minds, knowing the real root of our problems, the real root of our obstacles. This ultimately involves dealing with the idea of self itself—because it is actually from there that all forms of challenges derive.

I believe that both spiritual and non-spiritual people who are willing to work hard and make sacrifices for the benefit of others have a real potential for gaining freedom. Such people are able to put physical work, mental energy, and time into whatever it is they want to achieve. Because of this inner strength, if they happen to come across the right circumstances, the proper methods, and a genuine path, they are much closer to actual freedom.

True freedom is total freedom within yourself, gaining control of your body, speech, and mind. Then, almost regardless of external or outward circumstances, you are happy. You can do things with full conviction.

In terms of the body, this internal focus means, for example, watching your diet, taking care of your body, and doing other things to make you less prone to illness and help avoid many physical problems. But this is just an initial step.

Next, speech is very important. We have to communicate; we have no choice on this matter. So speech must have some ability—it's important to learn the ways and skills how to communicate, and how to convey your message adequately.

And finally, and most importantly, true freedom lies in your thoughts, your mind. Every action—whether it's a good or a bad one—will finally be decided by your intention, and by how you view things. So the mental factor is very, very important.

So, to gain freedom, you need to discipline your body, speech, and mind. By doing so, you will actually gain much more freedom than you might think.

In this way, discipline is actually not about restricting yourself – quite the contrary, you discipline yourself in order to gain freedom.

When you control your ego or yourself, you have all the freedom in the world. First of all, you realize the nature of ego, and by realizing that, you have no ego to be harmed or to be ashamed.

True freedom comes from conquering the self—the real root of our obstacles, our personal and global problems. I find it very interesting to deal with the self. It is liberating to work on inner experiences that we can do so much about, rather than focus on external circumstances alone, many of which we can have no control over. All challenges have their origin in their self. May you find the freedom you wish for in your selves.

# Peace

Peace is complete awareness. In this state of awareness, we cultivate and combine compassion and wisdom. In this state of awareness, we are alive, awake; we take responsibility for our actions. In this state, we are not driven by emotion; we control our emotions and actions. In this state, we are patient, nonviolent; we do not judge. In this state, we nurture our inner wealth—our innate values—and balance them with outer (material) wealth in a way that benefits all sentient beings. This is peace.

# Five Steps to a Wealthier Life

We all want to lead healthy and prosperous lives. The news headlines in the UK and around the world, however, are firmly focused on the activities of banks and bankers and the weakness of our global economy.

They paint a picture of wealth and prosperity defined by possessions and materialism alone. How do we lead wealthier lives, in ways that don't just involve accumulating money?

From the Buddhist point of view the root causes for the current crisis are certain human faults—in particular greed—and therefore I believe that the solution to the challenges we are facing today equally lies within the mind, or the consciousness of each individual.

If we ask ourselves what we, as individuals, can do to make a difference, I trust that change can be achieved by taking small steps to accumulate inner wealth. Fortunately, since there is a great number of human beings, if we add up the small steps that each individual takes, then within a very short time it will make a big difference—therefore, the strategy of taking small steps is both doable and effective.

First of all we have to be aware of the various types of means and resources that we have in our lives. Even ambition or desire can be used to develop inner wealth, if they are channelled in the proper way. For instance, if we have the desire and the ambition to generate contentment, then that is a good desire and a good ambition. So in this way we must make ourselves aware of various types of means at our disposal, and once we have done that, then an important method is that of comparing ourselves with others.

If we know how to properly apply the method of comparing ourselves with others we can extract a lot of inner wealth from that, too.

Often, we tend to compare ourselves with those who are wealthier, healthier, better-looking and generally better off, which leaves us feeling underprivileged and at a disadvantage—feelings which then become fertile ground for greed and desire.

If, on the other hand, we compare ourselves with those who are worse off, this will help us generate contentment and a sense of our own inner wealth and resources. Once again, in learning how to apply this method, it is best to proceed step by step.

## 1. Consider Animals

We might even start out by looking closely at the situation and suffering of animals and the limitations of their mental and verbal resources, and thus make ourselves aware of how much more freedom and scope for action we have as human beings.

## 2. Consider Those Less Fortunate

The next step would be to compare ourselves with those who are worse off—those who are poor, deprived, or sick, and once this step has been engrained, we can then go on to the next step, which is about learning how to compare ourselves with others who may not be sick or poor—maybe even healthier and wealthier than ourselves—but mentally unhappy or lacking in qualities such as compassion, courage, or generosity.

## 3. Question Crisis

This training may lead us to a point where we might re-examine the very idea that we are in a crisis. Maybe it's just a judgment on our part, based on the one-sided importance we have attached to material wealth. From our new perspective we may see that those who are poor in terms of material wealth might actually be quite wealthy in other areas.

## 4. Question Ourselves

We might be very critical of our own condition and think that we are very poor, but on closer examination this may not really be the case. Maybe we have been misjudging ourselves, but we will only realize that once we know how to compare.

## 5. Be Grateful

Finally, this way of training can bring us to a stage where when we feel that there is some sort of crisis, we can actually be thankful about it; it makes us think, it makes us reassess where we stand, and it can help us realize that we are being too judgmental about everything, especially ourselves, and make us appreciate that it wasn't as bad as we thought.

Therefore, I think that especially for us as "youth" it is important to constantly ask ourselves the question, "How much is enough?" both in relation to our material and non-material values. The world has come to a point where things are moving very fast; there is constant time pressure and we are often forced to grow up and mature very quickly and take on heavy responsibilities, and therefore it is all the more important to be very aware of our own state of mind as well as of our environment.

I will be going to England in a few days' time, and I look forward to meeting with young people and youth organisations during my visit there. The purpose of this blog is to share some of my thoughts with you, but also to improve my own understanding by learning about young people's ideas and concerns.

Therefore, it would be of great help if you could enlighten me with your thoughts by taking the Wealth of Europe Facebook poll.

# Are You Getting Richer or Poorer?

It goes without saying that a certain amount of material wealth—for example, those things related to food, clothing and shelter—is a necessity to sustain our life. Every individual has to work to survive, but when earning a living becomes the exclusive focus and priority of one's life, problems can arise. When we live to earn rather than earn to live, there can be problems of excess and greed.

However, there are also other forms of wealth, required not just to sustain the physical body, but to sustain and develop our mind. In this perspective, it may be interesting to look beyond the traditional ideas of financial wealth and really reflect on why our human species, among the many different types of existence, is so special and valuable. As a Buddhist practitioner and teacher, it is my hope and belief that Buddhism may have some interesting and valuable input to offer in this area. First of all, when trying to identify the causes for the present crisis from a Buddhist perspective, the root problems are certain human traits such as greed and laziness, all of which arise on the basis of ignorance.

It is one thing to cultivate just enough crops for your day-to-day needs. But when you start to collect crops, and start to stock up with the idea that you'll have less work and more money, this can sow the seeds of unchecked greed. So it is really important to be aware of certain human traits which bring a lot of unnecessary problems. Sometimes when we think we are getting richer, from a different perspective we are becoming poorer.

Though I never went to school myself (as the head of a lineage, I had a special type of education), I had the good fortune to learn about all this from my parents. Later on, when I got into Buddhist studies and teachings, I learned more and more about the faults and qualities of humanity, and that helped me to learn about life.

The inner wealth is our mind, our consciousness. I believe that this mind is like a wish-fulfilling jewel. If you know how to utilise this mind, it can produce the most beneficial effects. The best way to utilise and develop this mind is to absorb knowledge, and the most important kind of knowledge is the one that makes us a kind person; a decent person; a person worthy of respect. The qualities that make an individual kind, decent and respectable are qualities such as patience, generosity, and kindness. The good news is that we do not have to adopt or create these qualities, since they are already potentially there in all of us. In this way, the wealth lies latent within each and every one of us.

So all we need to do is give ourselves, every day, a bit of a reason to generate these qualities, bit by bit. If we do this, it will not make society perfect, but it will enable us to appreciate whatever circumstances we might face.

From a Buddhist perspective, we actually have to be grateful for obstacles because without them we never learn. It is thanks to difficulties and challenges that we can come up with solutions, some of which will work and some not. But even if they don't work it doesn't mean we should give up. It only means we should try again.

# Is It Necessary to Do Spiritual Practice Only Under Proper Guidance?

If the beginning of all knowledge is to know yourself and we have all the answers within ourselves, why is it so important to have a spiritual teacher?

We all have innate, unborn qualities. That is not to say that, in a Buddhist sense, we are already enlightened, but the seed of the potential is already planted inside each and every one of us. It is inherently present.

To really sit down and tell ourselves things, such as, "I am inherently pure and decent," can be difficult—although we can relate to these truths during unemotional moments. But if we have a hard time accepting these truths, when we are in crisis and have doubt in ourselves, then this is a clear sign that we do need someone to guide us; someone to show us; someone to explain and teach us what it is, and that it is like that.

In terms of the question of whether we need a teacher or not, it is not that we have to go to the end of the world to really find the answer. I believe it is right here, right now; we can just ask ourselves individually, "Do we really have the potential or not?" "Do we really understand the truth?" Or, we can change the terms by saying, "Do I know the nature of mind?" "Do I know the universe and phenomena?" and so on.

For this, we may need proper guidance. And then of course, there come many questions such as, "How to find an authentic guide?" and, "How do we know that that is the right path?" and so on. But for that I think it is important to focus on the basic qualities of the teachers or guides, and also use our own basic qualities to assess with a good degree of clarity, i.e. without emotion. So, whether Theravada teacher or Mahayana teacher, there are certain standards or certain basic qualities that he or she should require in order to guide.

# What Is a Good Practice to Start with for People Who Are New to Tibetan Buddhism?

Traditionally, when you begin Tibetan Buddhist practice, you take refuge in the Three Jewels, and start with the preliminary practices. But personally, I feel that if one is truly starting from step one, you must first have an attitude that, "I want to be decent. I want to draw from the inner wealth within." This is the foundation upon which you can then rely on the traditional aspects of the practices that are offered.

So the first step is reflection. Knowing that this inner wealth lies inside you, you may reflect on your own consciousness and try and see if there is an innate sense and understanding of cause and effect, an innate sense of aspiring for truth and peace. If we discover these things, then this is already the first non-traditional practice on the Tibetan Buddhist path.

To cultivate this inner wealth more, you can then begin with all the traditional practices, reflecting on questions that are grounded in logic and reason.

For example, is it logical that if you want to learn something that you must learn from someone who's experienced, and follow their path? And is it also logical to have a great, positive attitude? And is it relevant to have decency—be it in the way you think, the way you talk, and the way you behave? And does intention matter more than what you do?

If all of this seems reasonable and logical, then it is already a step on the path to realizing more of yourself and tapping into your inner wealth.

Then, you may also examine the traditional aspects of the practice, for example the Theravada, Mahayana, and Vajrayana traditional practices, and see if each one resonates with your own logic and reason, like the questions I just mentioned. By doing this, you won't just blindly jump into a way of life.

Otherwise, if you don't do any of these things at the beginning, then you may face the problem of feeling you have to adapt yourself to something completely new. Then it becomes a little bit unnatural. From time to time, or even from the start, you might have the feeling that it's not really according to your nature, according to your constitution—you're just adapting.

Let's say you are born and raised in the city and then go to live on a quiet, remote island. You could try very hard, but it would be a struggle to adapt. After some time it will not be easy - it's not easy at the beginning, it won't be easy in the middle, and it won't be easy in the end. Because in terms of every aspect, you would feel you are having to adapt to something that is not really according to your nature.

So in a similar way, you may have a sort of allergic reaction against the practice, which is not good! So instead, to adopt rather than adapt, you have to relate to it in a way as if there is already an inherent connection. Like for example, I am a Tibetan, but there is an inherent connection with East, West, South or North, simply because I'm a human being. And so in that way there is no difference at all. And then, just like that, there are so many similar things. There is no need to adapt!

I'm saying this because I think there is a risk or a danger, which is passive but has a lot of weight. It arises when one feels, "I am a human being, so I have emotions, and that's who I am. So why do I have to try to actually remove those emotions? If I do that, then I might just become a machine. And if spirituality is meant to do that, then do I really want spirituality?"

While the logic of this thinking is correct, it is applied in the wrong way. Emotion is not a part of you, it is just a temporary habit. You are not inherently angry, or inherently any emotion. Emotions pass. The path to spirituality is about discovering your true nature, tapping into your inner wealth.

Understanding this point almost automatically negates the idea that spirituality or practice is a way to alter a person's true nature.

For these reasons, reflecting on our motivations, logic, and reasons for practicing are important non-traditional first steps, before setting out on the more traditional Tibetan Buddhist path.

# How Can a Buddhist Best Lead a Normal, Non-Monastic Life?

The poem "Letter to a Friend" by Nagarjuna beautifully sets out some basic guidelines for a non-ordained person to live their life. But even if all these guidelines were followed, there would still be some challenges.

A great deal depends on the individual concerned, their karma and other factors. For example, some people may have the motivation, but perhaps lack the circumstances. Others may have the circumstances but perhaps lack the motivation—in terms of entering ordained life, of course. So it is really a hard thing to say how best to lead "a normal life," as everyone is different.

The monastic sangha is crucial to help ensure the Buddha Dharma's benefit for all sentient beings. Without it, I would say that it would be very, very difficult for the Buddha Dharma to flourish. I believe that this was one of the very first reasons why our historical Buddha Shakyamuni established the sangha. I don't think he intended to develop the monastic system to convert everyone. But, should an individual, according to their own aspiration, wish to access the Buddha Dharma and follow this path, then the sangha enables them to do that.

So, there are many helpful guidelines for non-monastic life in "Letter to a Friend" by Nagarjuna, though one should always be mindful of the benefits and importance of the sangha.

# Is It True That in Buddhism We Don't Believe in God?

It is a very interesting and important question, and a simple yes/no answer would not suffice. Therefore, a little elaboration is required.

In general, and in simple terms, happiness is what we all seek. It's in our nature.

Some people doubt whether happiness can be found from within.

Because of these doubts, this confusion, and lack of knowledge, these people look to external sources to find happiness. They try to find happiness, freedom, peace, and enlightenment through divine intervention, for example.

When uncertainties exist, it is somehow easier to project an external source of happiness rather than look within. Thus humanity has tried over millennia to find the source of happiness outside ourselves.

With innocent motivations, we have come up with

various outer sources of happiness. For example, religions, anti-religions, power, money, and so on. As we continue to struggle in our external search for happiness, our progress seems to be limited in some way.

What Buddha Shakyamuni suggests is that while we struggle in our endless search and pursuit for happiness, we forget to ask, "Could it be that happiness is gained from within?"

He brings into focus, for example, the impermanence of all phenomena, like the very experience of "today." If we truly investigate "today's" nature, down to the very last fraction of experience, we might find that it never lasts. It is therefore free of a truly existing essence of "today"—even though it manifests vividly, and even leads to the experience of "tomorrow." Today is constantly changing, forever in flux.

If we accept the impermanence of life and nature, we can see how the external search for happiness may face many challenges along the way. A fixed view of "today" may lead to a fear of the day passing into "yesterday," a fear of "tomorrow," and so on. When we accept the way things are, perhaps we could liberate ourselves from these fears, and find peace and happiness—from within. We might even enjoy this "today" without depending on outer means.

In short, it is very difficult for a Buddhist to claim that there is a belief or doctrine that truly exists, because of the idea of impermanence.

Therefore, the concept of a creator is not recommended.

Having said that, in Buddhism there is a belief system, but in the form of a guideline. For example, should the belief in the notion of "karma" (the law of cause and effect) support someone in being a decent person, then that belief is valid, but only within that specific framework. This does not imply that there is such a thing as a fixed karma or a truly existing karma.

When we embrace impermanence and look inside ourselves, we are able to free ourselves from fear and support each other in our universal search for happiness.

# Vesak or Buddha Jayanti

Buddha Purnima (also known as Vesak or Buddha Jayanti) is the most sacred of Buddhist festivals, marking three of the most important events in the life of Gautama Buddha: his birth, enlightenment, and Parinirvana.

It is a very special day for all practitioners of Buddhism, because it is the anniversary of three important events in Lord Buddha's life.

First of all, it is the anniversary of Lord Buddha being born in our world.

Secondly, under the Bodhi Tree, he attained what we all wish and hope to attain: perfect enlightenment. There are many different types of liberation known throughout the world, over the centuries and millennia—they all have their own philosophies, theories, conclusions, and ideas about various forms of liberation, but the one that Gautama attained under the Bodhi Tree is known as the perfect enlightenment, the absolute liberation. So that's the second event.

And the third one is known as the Parinirvana, meaning that the present conditions that we have—the external or outer conditions, which are the world we live in; the inner conditions, such as our thoughts and our own body; as well as the secret conditions, our own consciousness—that all of these are compounded phenomena, and from the moment something is compounded, it is a given that at one particular time whatever compounded phenomenon was there will be subject to impermanence; it will dissolve. And so, in order to demonstrate that, to show that, the Buddha passed away into perfect enlightenment, and in doing so he left with a great teaching, showing that all phenomena come to an end. It is neither good nor bad; it is natural.

So these three events sum up the whole teaching of the Dharma, everything that we as practitioners are trying to understand and achieve.

# What Is the Purpose of Taking the Sojong Vows on Buddha Purnima?

Buddha Purnima is an auspicious day. A precious day. A day that all of us celebrate—all of us as students of Buddha Shakyamuni. While the date of Buddha Purnima varies with different traditions, as Buddhists we all agree that during this month we celebrate the life of a person who was very precious and important to us.

So we celebrate Buddha's presence in our world: his birth, then, the most important aspect of the Buddha's activity, his enlightenment, and his Parinirvana, which is another important activity, one could say. All three of these aspects of Buddha's presence fall on this very day, as I'm sure you know.

So we celebrate this day according to our traditions, according to the way we feel it is special. But I'm not sure whether Buddha himself would have agreed with our method of celebrating this anniversary. This is simply because this was not the main purpose of his life or message.

Buddha's main purpose lay in the way in which he lived his life—whatever positive examples he could pass on. His life was his message. If we truly appreciate this, and at least aim to follow and apply this purpose in our own lives, then I think this is something that he would have liked.

Nevertheless, this tradition of celebration has been carried on for more than 2,500 years. Of course, it is our right, individually, and according to our customs, that we mark this special day in which ever way we feel appropriate. I believe that it is important that we mark this moment every year by doing something positive— something beneficial—just as we are doing today.

Right now, we are receiving the vow of Sojong. I think that this is exactly what the Buddha would have wished. In taking these vows—even if it's for a mere 24 hours—we become free of Samsaric duties. We are free of the conditioned Samsaric rules. We are liberated from disturbing emotions. We can think more clearly. We are able to understand how life functions. How we react. How we respond to one another. Most importantly, we understand how we are able to appreciate one another, because we create an atmosphere, an environment, in which we are free of disturbing emotions. And by doing so, the karmic cycle also reduces, opening up more space for developing compassion, understanding and loving kindness. There are so many beautiful benefits from creating this wonderful environment.

The taking of the Pratimoksha Vows is therefore not a way of restricting ourselves at all, but rather a way of opening ourselves up to many beautiful possibilities.

I believe the vows are of great benefit. They are designed to benefit not only ourselves but all sentient beings in a very practical, tangible way.

I say tangible because it is not something far away that we have to wait or wish for, but something we experience in the present moment. We experience the benefits while we obtain these vows—actually without having to do much ourselves. The vows benefit our mental attitude, and by doing so, they can even bring purity to our physical attributes, such as our speech or actions. So even if we were to gather the smallest of virtues, it would multiply to limitless ends.

Therefore, we must rejoice. We must rejoice for ourselves. We must rejoice for all sentient beings. And we must offer this as an offering to the Buddhas and bodhisattvas of the ten directions.

# Questions Concerning Pure View and the Ability to Discriminate

As the Buddha is omniscient, and we are aiming to reach the same wisdom of knowing everything exactly as it is, why should be "superimpose" a pure view on something that we know to be a fact? For example, if someone has certain faults, is pure view about wiping away/ignoring these faults about the person, rather than having an accurate assessment of that person?

In a Buddhist context, the longer we spend on the path as a practitioner, the more important it is to explore the subject of pure view.

The act of judging or the ability to judge is a delicate matter. Before we are able to judge a situation, we first need to be aware of every fact, every angle of that situation. But, again, it is a delicate matter. We are somehow never quite sure that every angle has been covered. Our instinct, and indeed our doubts, can be helpful tools to enable us to assess things.

I believe that the very act of struggling to prove a point is a type of judgement. However, when we do judge, I think it is important that the motivation is for the benefit of others, rather than proving a point for ourselves. By putting our point across, it may improve the quality and ability for all to assess a situation.

While judging through complete understanding may be considered part of the Buddhist path, the development of pure view may be considered as the path within the path.

The higher the level of purity in our view, the lower the burden of having to judge at all. When we have pure view, we are able to see the facts as they are—there is no need to judge or say something is "like this" or "like that." When we have pure view, we do not need to go around struggling to prove something. It is what it is.

As long as we have pure view, there is less room for mistakes, and everything becomes clearer. Questions might arise about whether or not we all have this potential for pure view, but those with pure view understand that we all have this potential. Those with pure view have a very broad, a panoramic, perspective, let's say. Again, the need to judge, either oneself or others, is no longer present.

Now, when it comes to benefiting others, let's say in the case of a bodhisattva, the purpose of his or her life is to guide and support others. To be able to do this, you first need to be a good guide yourself. Part of being a good guide is to make things clear for others, which in some ways entails an element of judgement. In the case of a bodhisattva, therefore, some judgement comes into play, even when there is pure view.

# What Is Stopping Me from Realizing My True Nature, Buddha-Nature?

Perhaps it is a lack of a sense of adventure that is holding us back from realizing our true nature. It is easy to get used to the mundane life, the daily routines. As a result, we don't want to let go of our familiar atmosphere, the life that we are used to. We are missing a sense of adventure.

I think this is rooted in a deep fear: a fear of facing ourselves; a fear of knowing exactly who we are. It is almost like saying we fear looking at ourselves in the mirror and seeing our own reflections.

Of course, the trouble, or rather the challenge, comes from believing that the mundane elements of our lives somehow define who we are. The errors, the mistakes, the hardships and challenges that we have faced, can sometimes feel like they become a part of us. They hold us back, leaving their mark, sometimes even a sense of trauma. But these experiences are not part of our true nature. In fact, in some ways they can hold us back from seeing our true selves.

Over the years, this kind of habitual pattern can somehow make us not believe in our own true nature, and feel that it is just wishful thinking that our true nature is different—a hopeful dream! So, I think this is what we have to overcome.

So that's why we have to have great courage, and be a bit stern—even a bit stubborn—to really face ourselves.

As practitioners, we will all be faced to some degree by the emotions, challenges and obstacles we experience in life. Without truly facing them, we will never ever realize our true nature.

When we really face ourselves, when we see our true reflections in the mirror, we see that the errors of this life are manifestations of none other than karma and *klesha*. We are then able to accept the way things are in quite an efficient way. It is almost as though we are tagging or categorizing our mundane experiences. Once we have somehow put them in their own places, we have nothing to see but ourselves and our true potential. This takes courage. It takes courage to face the fear of the past—to overcome the error of seeing our negative experiences as part of our true selves—but we need to do this in order to to help realize our true nature.

# Emptiness

Interdependence is another way to introduce the idea of emptiness. When we talk about emptiness, it can draw a lot of confused and unwanted thoughts, fear, and all kinds of unnecessary conclusions. So that's why another way of interpreting it, another way of saying it, is by using the word interdependence. Because when you say "interdependence," it naturally shows that there is no one, separate entity that is autonomous or independent. Yes, that each of the components must depend on another and therefore there is no singular entity. This is emptiness. Everything happens due to a cause and due to that cause there is that effect. And also between the cause and effect, there also need to be the conditions, so you see, all these chains of dependency. So that is another way of showing that everything is impermanent, everything is empty.

# Other Titles by Rabsel Éditions

A Path of Wisdom
Jigme Rinpoche *2012*

The Karmapa Prophecies
Sylvia Wong *2016*

The Handbook of Ordinary Heroes
Lama Jigme Rinpoche *2016*

Being Present:
*A Skill Worth Developing*
Anila Trinlé *2017*

Printed in May 2017
by Pulsio

Edition Number: 0027
Legal Deposit: May 2017
Printed in Bulgaria